—SPACE—
WEAPONS

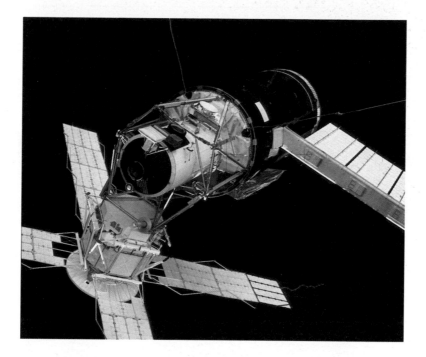

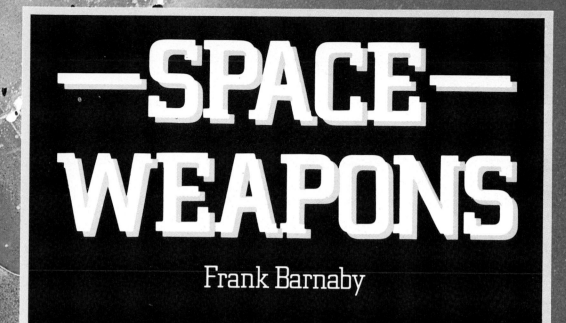

SPACE WEAPONS

Frank Barnaby

GALLERY BOOKS
An Imprint of W. H. Smith Publishers Inc.
112 Madison Avenue
New York City 10016

CONTENTS

The book was devised and produced by
Multimedia Publications (UK) Ltd.

Editor Jeff Groman
Design Mick Hodson
Picture Research Military Archive and Research Services; Picture Research, Washington
Production Arnon Orbach

Copyright © Multimedia Publications (UK) Ltd. 1984

ISBN 0 8317 7951 9

First published in the United States of America by
Gallery Books, an imprint of W.H. Smith Publishers Inc.,
112 Madison Avenue, New York, NY 10016.

Originated by D S Colour International Ltd, London

Printed by Sagdos, Milan

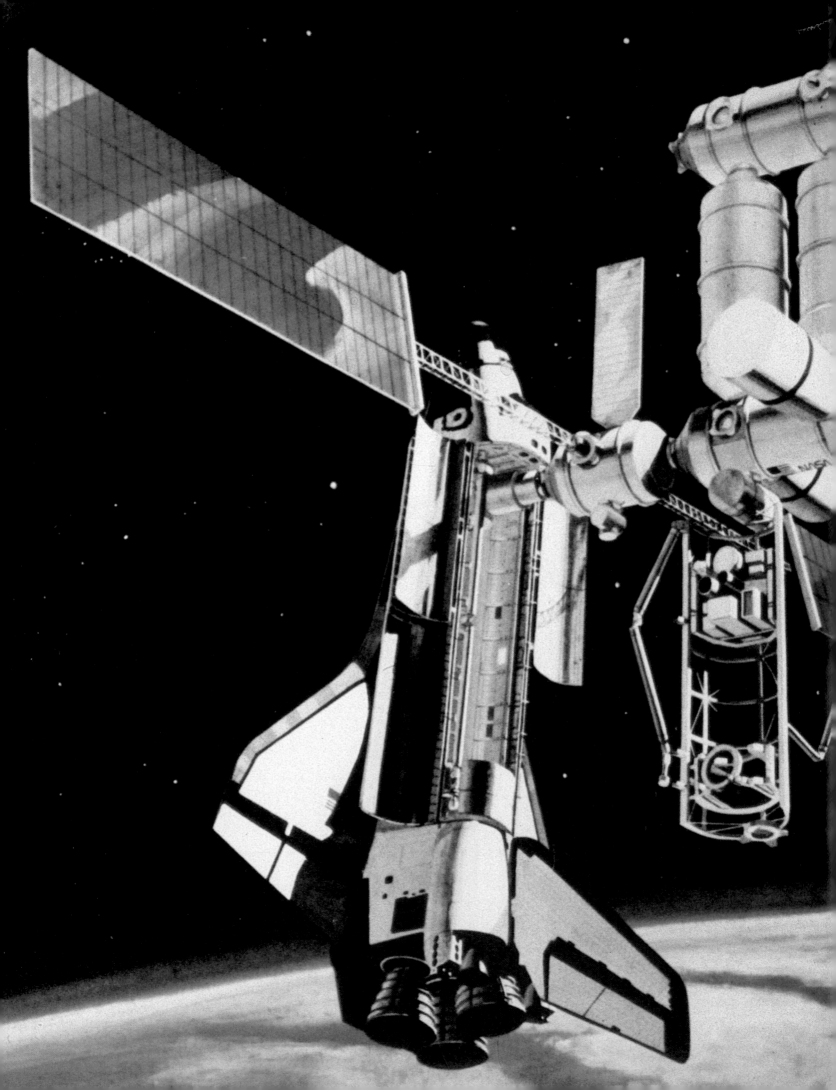

INTRODUCTION

President Reagan unveiled his 'Star Wars' plan in a speech on 23rd March, 1983. 'I call upon the scientific community who gave us nuclear weapons,' the President said, 'to turn their great talents to the cause of mankind and world peace: to give us the means of rendering these nuclear weapons impotent and obsolete.' President Reagan's plan is to use very exotic weapons, like high-energy lasers, on 'space battle-stations' as part of a defense system that has the job of destroying in-flight Soviet ballistic missiles sent to attack the United States.

The President's call for an armada of space battle-stations to defend the USA against nuclear attack brings home the extent to which space has become militarized. Since 1957, when the space age began, over 2,000 military satellites have been launched into space. This means that three out of every four satellites put into space are for military use.

About 100 military satellites are launched each year; about 85 by the USSR and about 15 by the USA. The different numbers are explained by the fact that American satellites are usually able to stay up in space for longer periods than Soviet ones. A typical US Big Bird satellite, for example, stays in space for about 200 days, whereas a typical Soviet Cosmos satellite comes down after about 30 days.

Satellites perform a variety of tasks for the military: reconnaissance, weather forecasting, navigation, and communications. Photographic reconnaissance satellites are the 'eyes' of the military in space; electronic surveillance satellites are its 'ears'. The latter spacecraft carry equipment to detect and monitor the enemy's radar signals, his radio communications, and even his telephone communications. Their missions are the most secret of all space activities.

Anti-satellite Weaponry

The military in the advanced countries are now dependent on satellites. No wonder that both the USA and the USSR see the other side's satellites as vital military targets. Both superpowers are working energetically to develop weapons to attack and destroy each other's satellites in space. These are called anti-satellite, or ASAT, weapons.

ASAT weapons include hunter-killer satellites, which intercept and destroy enemy satellites in orbit, and high-energy lasers, stationed in space for the same reason. The high-energy laser beam is the link between anti-satellite weapons and the anti-ballistic missiles of Reagan's 'Star Wars' proposal.

Laser beams are essentially beams of light. When you turn on an electric light bulb, the light streams out of the bulb in all directions, illuminating the whole room. But light from the instrument known as a 'laser' goes in one direction only. An enormous amount of energy can be concentrated in a laser beam — enough to cut a hole through a steel block a few inches thick. If a high-energy laser beam hits a ballistic missile or its warhead it can cause enough damage to make it ineffective. It can also destroy an enemy satellite in orbit. Lasers are, therefore, important components of many space weapons.

The use of space weapons was predicted twenty years ago by President Kennedy. 'Only if the United States occupies a position of pre-eminence,' Kennedy said about space activities, 'can we help decide whether this new ocean will be a sea of peace, or a terrifying theater of war.'

In 1984, President Reagan instructed NASA to develop a permanently manned space station. Congress has provided initial funding for the project. It is expected that space stations will be developed within a decade. Permanently manned space stations obviously have considerable military potential and their deployment may well complete the militarization of space. The USA and the USSR may, however, negotiate treaties to limit military activity in space.

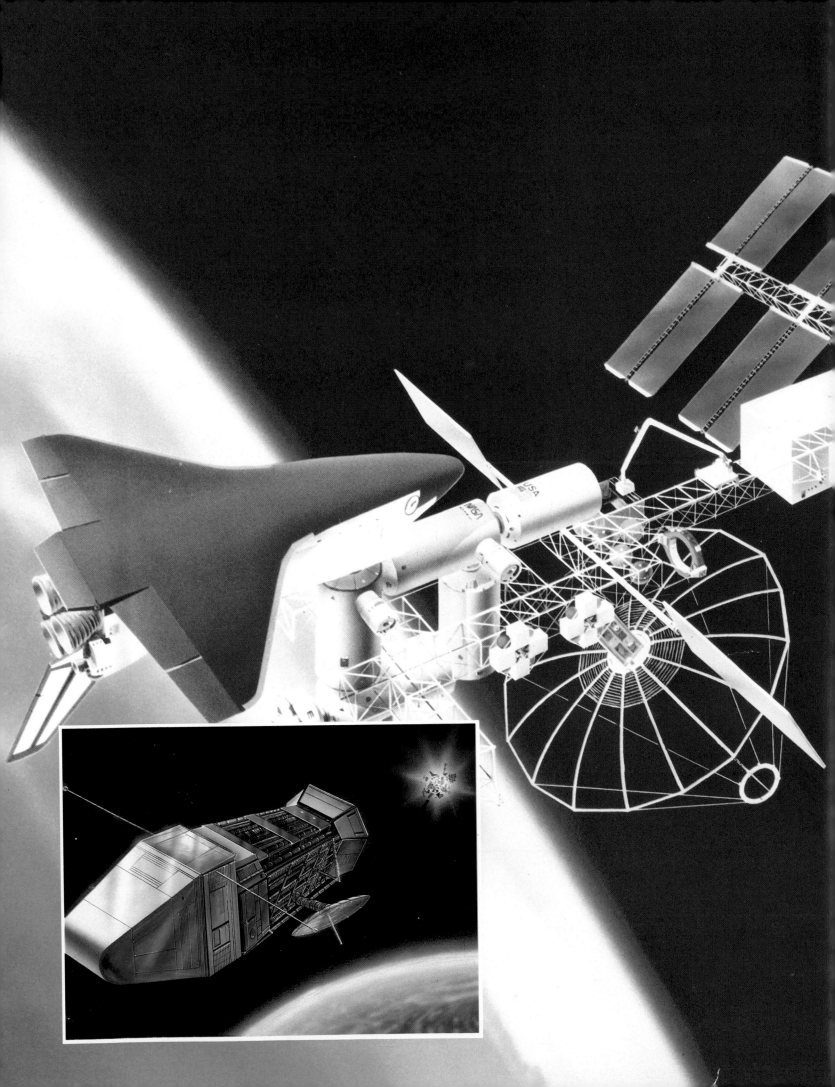

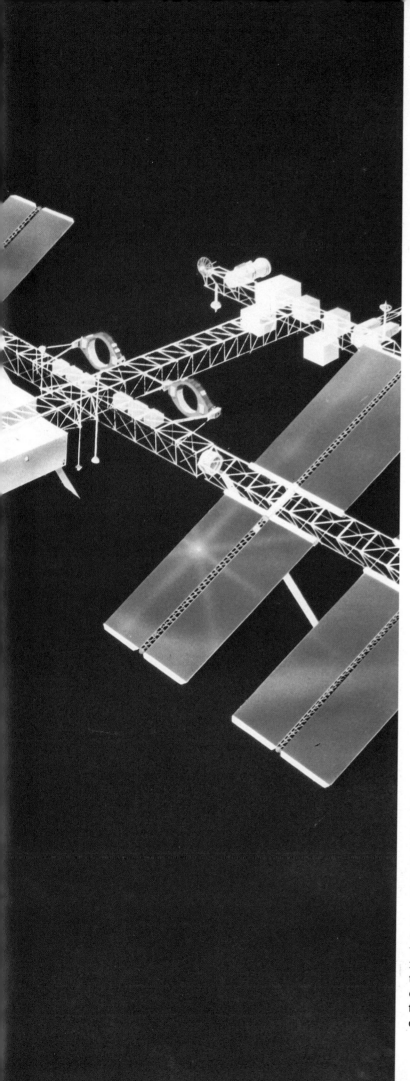

Reusable Hardware in Space

The deployment of weapons in space will be made easier by the space shuttle. A large percentage of future US shuttle flights will be operated for the Pentagon. And it is likely that the Soviets will soon launch a reusable manned space shuttle, probably from the Soviet space launch site at Tyuratam.

That the US military is serious about the future exploitation of space is shown by the formation of a new Space Command by the US Air Force to integrate all military space activities. The Command's Consolidated Space Operations Center, at Peterson Air Force Base, near Colorado Springs, will control and manage space flight operations. The US Air Force is also building its own shuttle launch and landing site at the Vandenberg Air Force Base, from where most US military satellites are now launched.

The space shuttle will certainly make it easier to carry out manned activities in outer space. In a few years there will probably be hundreds of people in space, many being occupied with military duties.

The USSR has energetically pursued its manned space program for more than twenty years now and has maintained its lead over the USA. Not only was a Soviet cosmonaut the first man to orbit the Earth but the Soviet Union was the first nation to launch a man into space.

Most manned space flights have been successful but we should not forget the spacemen who sacrificed their lives. Three American astronauts and one Soviet cosmonaut died in 1967 and three other Soviet cosmonauts died in 1971.

Military Space Stations

The Soviets are busily constructing space stations; Soyuz satellites transfer people and goods between Earth and Salyut space stations. The USA intends to build a large space station with materials transported in space shuttle flights.

Space stations could be used for many military purposes, including the deployment of weapons in space and the stationing of troops. Full-scale military bases in space may have become commonplace by the next century.

We usually think that the USA and the USSR are the only military powers in space. But four other countries have launched their own spacecraft. France, China, Japan and India are all space powers. And there are other countries, such as Brazil, that have advanced high-altitude rocket programs in which rockets are fired into the upper atmosphere for scientific experiments. These countries will no doubt eventually develop their own space-launchers and put satellites into space. Many of these satellites will be used to support military activities.

Countries that can launch satellites can also operate ballistic missiles. These are themselves space weapons because a large fraction of their trajectories pass through space. Membership of the space club is without doubt a major military status symbol.

Left, main picture: The Soviets have already had much experience with manned space stations, dating from April 1971 when the space shuttle Salyut 1 was put into orbit. In the past few years, several new prototypes of Soviet space ships have been tested; manned space missions have taken place at the rate of 3 or 4 a year. Cosmonauts from Poland, Czechoslovakia, East Germany, Bulgaria, Hungary, Vietnam, Cuba, Romania, Mongolia, and India have participated in Soviet space flights.

Left, inset: Exotic weapons like this particle beam weapon are being considered for deployment in space. Typically, electrons or protons would be brought up to near the speed of light and fired at an enemy nuclear warhead in space. The beam would either physically damage the warhead or heat it enough to destroy it. Particle beam weapons could also be used against high-flying aircraft. Some scientists believe that these massive weapons will become available in 20 years or so; other scientists doubt their feasibility.

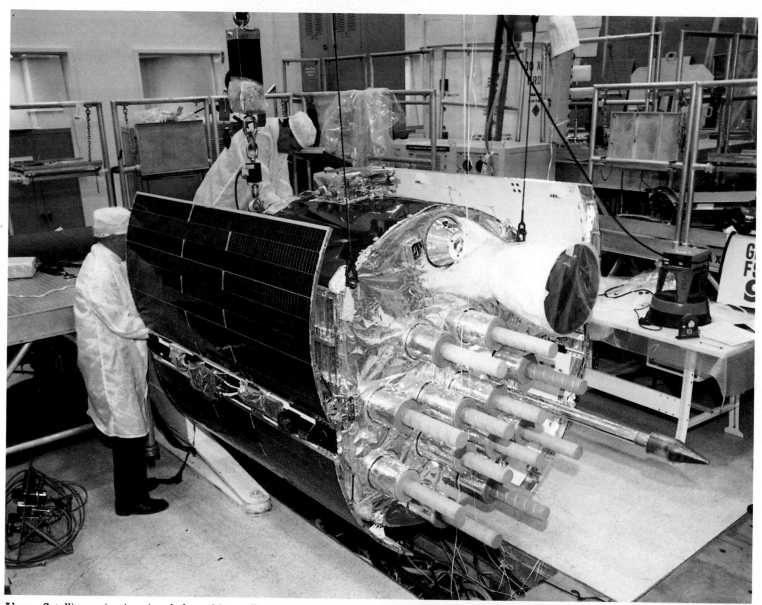

Above: Satellite navigation signals from this satellite were successfully beamed back and forth to Earth in initial tests of the US Global Position System satellite. The entire space navigation system, called NAVSTAR, will be based on 18 satellites in orbits 10,900 miles (17,540 km) above the Earth. The space-based radio navigation system will provide highly accurate position, speed, and time information for civilian ships and aircraft. It will also send out even more accurate information for military purposes, including the guidance of missiles in flight. The NAVSTAR satellite system will greatly increase US military capabilities by improving the accuracy and reliability of weapon delivery. The civilian navigation signals will be available to any user but the military signals will be coded and not generally available. The entire system should be operational by 1988.

Left: An Atlas rocket in position by its gantry. Some 10 types of non-reusable launchers have been developed by the USA to put satellites into orbit. At least three of these launchers — Atlas, Thor, and Titan — were derived from military ballistic missiles. The Atlas rocket has been crucial to the development of US space activities right from the time they began in 1958 and original design considerations can be dated back to 1948. Atlas rockets were used as boosters for early US manned space flights.

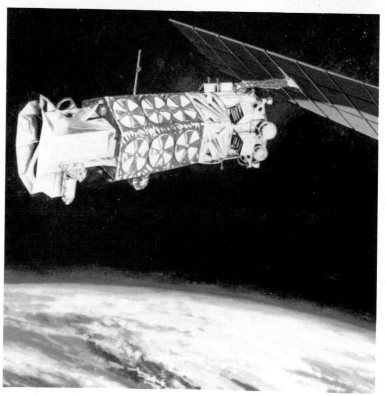

Right: An artist's concept of a military meteorological satellite. Weather forecasting is an important military activity in space.

Above: The Delta launch vehicle, with nine strap-on boosters, is a typical space-age work-horse. It has been used by the USA since 1960 to launch dozens of satellites. Between 1975 and 1978, for example, Delta launchers put 40 satellites into orbit — an average of nearly one a month.

Right: This Atlas Centaur is about to launch a military communications satellite called FLTSATCOM, which stands for Fleet Satellite Communication System. These spacecraft are used for communications mainly by the US Navy. Typically, a FLTSATCOM satellite, which weighs about two tons, is in a stationary orbit above the equator at an altitude of 22,250 miles (36,000 km). The military forces of the superpowers now rely on satellites for their communications, their 'ears' in space. Communications satellites complement reconnaissance satellites — the military's 'eyes' in space.

Left, inset: An Atlas rocket leaves a plume around its nose cone area in a successful launch trajectory.

Left, main picture: But not all launches are successful. This Delta launch vehicle carrying a communications satellite malfunctioned in flight and the rocket broke up some 102 seconds into its mission. The destruct action was initiated by the test range controllers when it was obvious that the mission could not succeed.

Right: Ford Aerospace and Communications Corporation technicians testing a Japanese communications satellite prior to launch. The satellite programme is a joint effort by Mitsubishi Electric Company of Japan and Ford Aerospace to develop Japan's space programme. Japan is one of a number of countries, including also India and Brazil, which have developed space capabilities from peaceful high-altitude rocket technology. In the case of the USA, the USSR, France, and China, space launchers were developed from military missiles. Japan and India, by launching satellites using their own space launchers, have demonstrated a capability to produce also intercontinental ballistic missiles. Japan, India, and Brazil are among the countries which could, if they took the political decision to do so, produce nuclear warheads for missiles. More and more countries will achieve this combination of space and nuclear capabilities, a proliferation which will have profound consequences for world security.

Below: India's combined communications and meteorological satellite. India has launched two satellites, in July 1980 and May 1981. The second satellite developed a problem and did not achieve its planned orbit; it re-entered the Earth's atmosphere after 10 days in space.

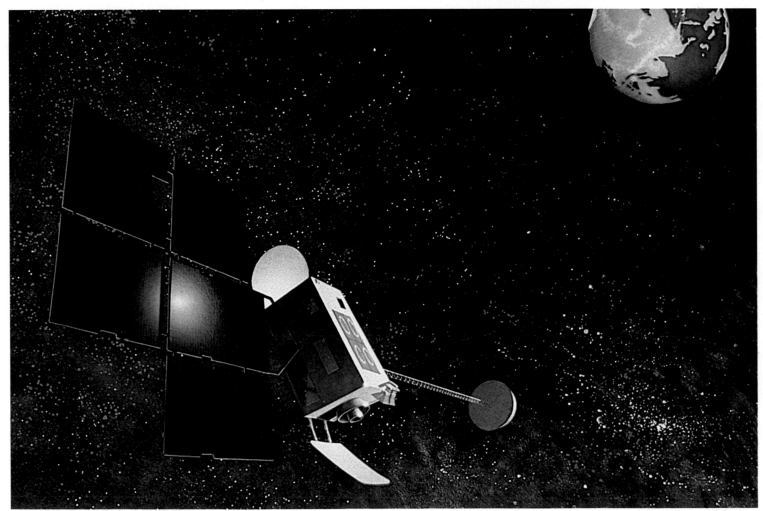

Right, cut out: A Horizontal Take-Off and Land Satellite Launcher, a technological break-through achieved by the British Aerospace Company. Liquid oxygen is not required to propel the vehicle. The vehicle, propelled by a combination of air breathing and rocket propulsion, would take off horizontally from a runway and could carry payloads into space of up to seven tons.

Right, middle: The space shuttle is more economical, more efficient, and more flexible than non-reusable space launchers. Flights on the space shuttle are less stressful for the crew who will, therefore, be able to build large constructions in space.

Below: Space stations may be used as bases to station troops or deploy weapons. Enemy countries may be attacked by, for example, weapons on space stations fired by signals from the ground.

Far right: Space is now a major factor in the arms race. Huge sums of money are being used for the exploitation of space. The establishment of a permanent manned space station is likely to run into $10 billion or so. Both superpowers seem prepared to spend such sums on space stations. The USA has initiated the development of a permanent manned space station and the USSR is reported to have begun testing a modular space station.

CHAPTER 1

SPACE WEAPONS

Weapons in space date back to the last years of World War II when the Germans invented the V-2 missile. Part of the trajectory of V-2s on their way to their targets in, for example, London, England, was spent in space. The early V-2s typically reached a height of about 60 miles (100 km) – the greatest height reached by any man-made object up to that time.

Age of the IBMs

The success of the German V-2 stimulated the superpowers to develop intercontinental ballistic missiles. Whereas the range of the V-2 was about 200 miles (320 km), the range of intercontinental ballistic missiles is typically about 8,000 miles (12,900 km). On normal trajectories these missiles reach heights of some 100 miles (160 km), taking them well into space.

In 1957, the USSR launched by far the largest rocket the world had ever seen. Its height was 100 feet (30 meters) and it weighed 300 tons (305 tonnes). The rocket, called Sapwood in the West, was powered by no fewer than 32 engines, and its duties included putting the first Sputnik into orbit. Another launched Yuri Gagarin into space. Others were used to put up a variety of satellites, many for military purposes, and further examples were used by the military as ballistic missiles.

But rocket technology advanced so rapidly after the late 1950s that the gigantic Soviet Sapwood rockets soon became museum pieces. A rocket with 32 large engines became unthinkable. Brute force gave way to sophistication.

American rockets were also multipurpose, used for military missiles and as launchers of space vehicles, many of which, in turn, had military missions. Thor, Atlas and Titan rockets have been the work-horses of US space activities; they were all derived from military ballistic missiles.

In the past 25 years, the USA and the USSR have deployed large numbers of strategic ballistic missiles, while Britain, France and China have also become strategic nuclear powers. And India and Japan have developed launchers to put spacecraft into orbit; these rockets could easily be used as military missiles to deliver warheads over ranges of several thousand miles. Altogether, there are more than 4,100 strategic ballistic missiles in the world today.

Far left: A Titan II intercontinental ballistic missile (ICBM) of the US Air Force being test fired. The missile is over 100 ft (30 meters) long and is the biggest missile ever deployed by the West. Titan II has a launch weight of 330,000 lb (150,000 kg) and can carry a 9-megaton (the equivalent in destructive power of 9 million tons of TNT) nuclear warhead a distance of 9,325 miles (15,000 km). Soviet ICBMs are even bigger; the SS-18 ICBM has a launch weight of about 485,000 lb (220,000 kg) and a range of about 7,500 miles (12,000 km). (The SS-18 can carry a 25 megaton nuclear warhead.) The Titan II became operational in 1963; 54 of them were deployed. Two Titans exploded in their silos and the missiles are now being withdrawn.

Left, inset: A Titan II underground silo complex.

Left: A launch of a Minuteman III from its silo. This is the most modern American ICBM and the world's most accurate strategic ballistic missile. Currently 550 of these ICBMs are deployed at US Air Force bases at Malmstrom, Montana; Minot, North Dakota; Warren, Wyoming; and Grand Forks, North Dakota. They form the backbone of American land-based strategic forces. Each Minuteman III carries three warheads which can be fired at separate targets, hundreds of miles apart. Each warhead can have an explosive power equivalent to that of 330,000 tons of TNT. The range is over 8,000 miles (13,000 km). Because of the increased accuracy of ICBMs, each side is now able to destroy the other's ICBMs in their silos by a sudden attack. Fixed land-based strategic missiles can, therefore, be regarded as obsolete.

Beating the Radar

Although most missiles would travel through space on a ballistic trajectory, similar in shape to the path of a stone, some may be designed to stay longer in space. Thus the Soviet SS-9 Scarp missile was able to fly on a fractional orbit and was called the fractional orbital bombardment system. The idea was to confuse the American radars that give warning of an enemy missile attack.

When these radars were installed it was assumed that a Soviet missile attack against the USA would come from the east, with the Soviet missiles following ordinary ballistic trajectories. A fractional orbital system, however, would be sent round the other way and approach the USA from the west, a direction in which the radars would not be looking.

A Soviet fractional orbital bombardment system would be fired into space and travel in an orbit which would take it eastwards from the Soviet Union. When the missile had completed just over half its orbit it would find itself over the USA. The warhead would then be fired onto its target in the USA. In this way, the warheads carried by fractional orbital missiles could creep in behind the American radars and attack targets in the USA without warning.

The problem with the fractional orbital systems is that they are rather inaccurate – and these days it is accuracy that counts. It is not known whether there are any fractional orbital missiles still in operation.

The launchers that have been mentioned in this chapter so far can only be used once. But we have now entered a new era of the space age: the era of the reusable launcher. This began on 12th April, 1981, when the first US space shuttle was launched.

Space Shuttle

The space shuttle, which normally flies in an orbit about 150 to 180 miles (240 to 290 km) above the Earth, can place satellites into orbit, snatch satellites out of their orbits and repair and service satellites in orbit. It could also be used to send a satellite on its way into a very high orbit, or send a satellite into an 'escape' trajectory that would allow it to get right away from the Earth and travel on and on through space. The shuttle's ability to 'kidnap' a Soviet satellite from its orbit means that it can be seen as the ultimate anti-satellite weapon.

The Soviets are also experimenting with reusable launchers. Delta-winged re-entry vehicles have been launched into orbits about 120 miles high (193 km) and recovered after spending some time in orbit. Cosmos 1517, for example, was a delta-winged re-entry vehicle launched on 27th December, 1983, into an orbit and recovered in the Black Sea after spending about one and a half hours in space. Soviet manned flights with this type of reusable space vehicle are expected to begin soon.

The Soviet and American military could use space shuttles for a number of purposes. One obvious use is to transport into space equipment needed for the development of space weapons. They could also be used to transport materials to build space battle-stations equipped with, for example, high-energy lasers. Large structures built in space could be used as platforms for launching weapons at targets on Earth or for stationing troops in space.

By 1988, 72 space shuttle flights are planned. About one-third of them will carry military payloads. The superpowers are obviously well aware of the new opportunities for military activities in space.

Far left: The launch of a US Polaris submarine-launched ballistic missile (SLBM) from a submerged strategic nuclear submarine. These missiles have been replaced by the more modern Poseidon SLBMs.

Left: The launch of a US Trident SLBM from the strategic nuclear submarine, the USS *Francis Scott Key*. The Trident is the world's most modern SLBM. There are 568 Poseidon and Trident SLBMs in the US arsenal, the missiles are carried on 30 strategic nuclear submarines. Each Trident SLBM carries, on average, 8 warheads; each warhead can attack separate targets at a range of about 4,500 miles. Each Trident strategic nuclear submarine carries 24 Trident SLBMs. Two Trident submarines on station could destroy every Soviet city with a population greater than 150,000 people. Two Soviet strategic nuclear submarines on station could, of couse, do similar damage to the United States. The Soviets operate 62 such submarines.

Above: Countries other than the USA and the USSR operate significant strategic nuclear forces. The nuclear forces of France, the UK, and China are, however, much smaller than those of the USA and the USSR. Whereas the two superpowers each have about 25,000 nuclear weapons, the nuclear arsenals of the other three nuclear powers each contain about 800 nuclear weapons. This picture shows the test firing of a French land-based strategic ballistic missile.

Left, inset bottom: The test launch of a US Pershing II land-based tactical ballistic missile from White Sands Missile Range. Tactical nuclear weapons generally have a shorter range and carry less powerful nuclear warheads than strategic ballistic missiles. About 16,000 of the 25,000 American nuclear weapons are tactical; the Soviets have about the same number of nuclear weapons as the Americans. The Pershing II is the world's most accurate missile; it has an accuracy of about 160 ft (50 meters) over a range of about 1,000 miles (16,000 km). The missiles, carrying nuclear warheads, are being deployed in West Germany.

Left, inset top: The British and French operate submarine-launched ballistic missiles. This is a French MSBS-MI SLBM being launched from underwater. Each missile has a range of 1,550 miles (2,500 km). The French operate five strategic nuclear submarines and a sixth is planned; the British operate four strategic nuclear submarines. Each British and French strategic nuclear submarine carries 16 SLBMs. On average, the British and French navies each have at sea one of their strategic nuclear submarines; the others are in port to rest the crews or for maintenance.

Main picture: The placing of weapons and satellites in space will be made much easier by the space shuttle. This picture shows a launching of the Columbia space shuttle from the Kennedy Space Center in Florida. On this flight the shuttle carried a crew of six into space.

Above: A crew member takes a 'walk' in space.

Left: The space shuttle consists of the orbiter, the external tank, and two solid-fuelled rocket boosters. The orbiter carries the crew and payload. The cargo, which may include, for example, a military satellite, is carried in a bay 60 feet long and 15 feet in diameter. The bay is flexible enough to carry unmanned spacecraft in many shapes. A typical shuttle mission lasts from 7 to 30 days. The shuttle is launched by igniting the main engines and the boosters simultaneously; the power rockets the shuttle from the launch pad. At a predetermined point, the two solid rocket boosters separate from the orbiter and parachute to the sea. They are picked up and used again. The orbiter continues into space, jettisoning its external propellant tank just before orbiting. The tank breaks up when it enters the Earth's atmosphere. After its mission, the orbiter lands like an aeroplane on a runway at the Kennedy Space Center or Vandenberg Air Force Base.

Far left, inset: More and more Soviet and American cosmonauts and astronauts are becoming experienced at working in space outside their spacecraft. The operations they perform are called extra-vehicular activity (EVA). EVA is necessary for such missions as retrieving and repairing or maintaining satellites in space and building space stations. Spacemen can be provided with small rockets so that they can maneuver themselves in space without any connection with the shuttle vehicle.

Left, inset: One of the jobs of the astronauts is to empty the cargo and, when necessary, launch objects into space orbit. The shuttle crew would be particularly busy if they were delivering material to construct or supply a space battle-station.

Main picture: Two American astronauts examine the handrail system on the bulkhead of the space shuttle Challenger during a long period of activity outside the shuttle. The vertical stabilizer and the orbital maneuvering system (OMS) frame a portion of Mexico's state of Jalisco below. The purpose of the OMS is to adjust the shuttle's path in orbit to allow it to maneuver. This is necessary for rendezvousing with other spacecraft, like military satellites, and at the end of the mission, for slowing down so as to head back to Earth. The greater the maneuverability of the shuttle the more tasks it will be able to perform; maneuverability is particularly important for many military missions.

Above: The first flight of the Columbia space shuttle took place in 1981. Since then three other models − Challenger, Discoverer, and Atlantis − have been developed. Depending on the orbit chosen the US space shuttle can carry into orbit up to heights of about 400 miles (650 km) a load ranging from 10 tons to 30 tons. About one-third of the 500 or so experiments planned for space shuttle flights up to 1994 will have military aims. To assist some of these missions, the Pentagon has ordered a booster to the space shuttle vehicle that can carry payloads of up to 2.2 tons into high orbits, up to 22,000 miles (36,000 km). This booster has already been developed. One military task of the space shuttle will be to service military satellites. This picture shows the shuttle deploying a satellite back into orbit.

Right: Military space stations for deploying weapon systems will probably be modular in design, as shown in this concept.

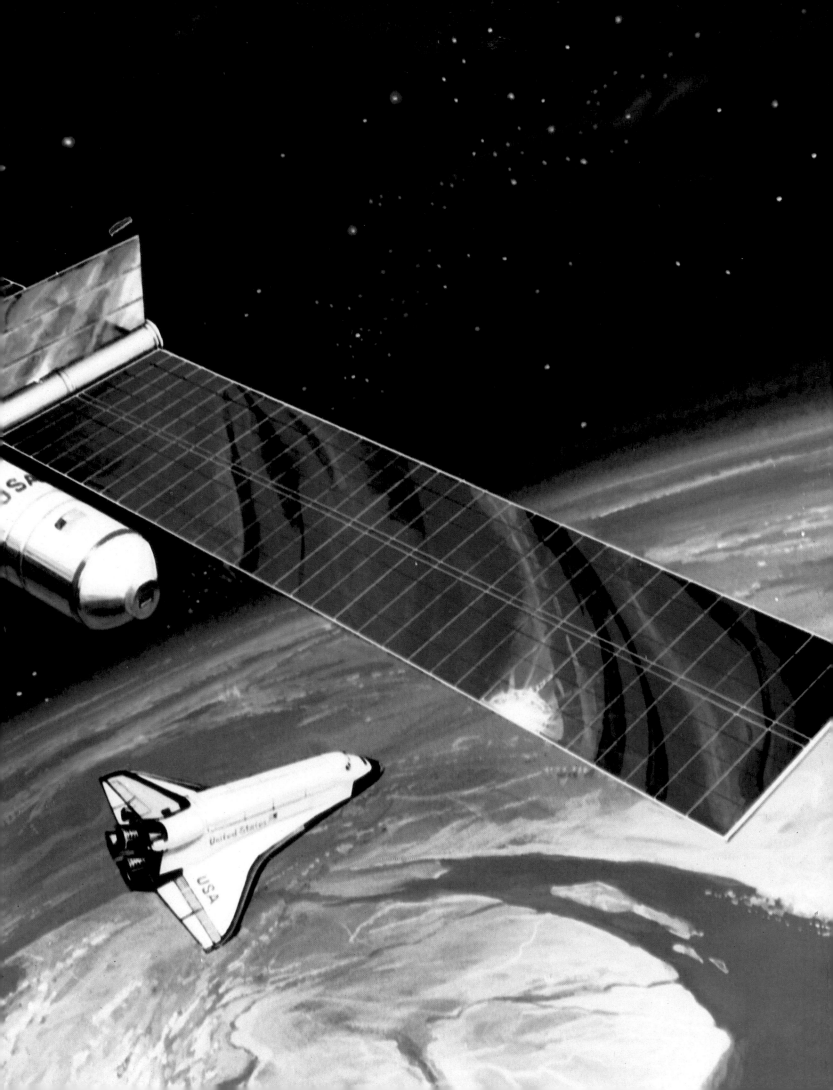

Main picture: American space scientists and engineers have designed a system for colonizing a permanent community in space. The picture shows a possible space colony that looks like a giant wheel in space. The outer 'tyre' is a radiation shield built of compressed cinder-block-like lunar material. The central hub contains a docking station and communication antenna and equipment. Six spokes connect the hub with the circular outer wheel and provide entry and exit to living quarters and areas for gowing food. To simulate the Earth's normal gravity the entire station rotates at one revolution a minute about the central hub. The polished disc that hangs suspended near the wheel is a floating mirror panel that reflects sunlight down onto the slanted panels and into shields that screen out radiation from deep space. The military applications of such a space colony would include reconnaissance and communication activities but it could also be used as a full-scale military base.

Left, inset and above: Military space stations may come in a large number of shapes and sizes. Few people realise that the exploitation of space is only just beginning. Much technological progress will occur before the year 2000. Some experts believe that the USA and the USSR will build space stations weighing about 100 tons by the early 1990s and space stations weighing over 1,000 tons by the end of the century. The successor to the space shuttle, the heavy-lift vehicle, will be able to transport large masses into space and allow the construction of large space stations.

CHAPTER 2

SPIES IN SPACE

The most obvious military use of a satellite is as a weapon in the espionage war between the USA and USSR. Overhead methods of espionage came of age in the mid-1950s with the use of the high-flying spy plane, the U-2. For the first time in military history, cameras on U-2s were able to photograph such huge areas of the Earth's surface that it became feasible to photograph entire continents. The superpowers from then on have found it very difficult to hide activities of any scale from each other.

Espionage by Satellite

The U-2 spy plane was followed by the American SR-71 reconnaissance aircraft. Both of these types of aircraft are able to fly at altitudes of about 15 miles (24 km) to take their photographs. The problem with using them for espionage is that it takes quite a time for the aircraft to complete its flight and unload the film, and then for the analysts to develop and analyse the pictures. Satellites flying at much higher altitudes are, in most cases, able to do the job more efficiently than high-flying spy aircraft.

Until recently, all photographic reconnaissance satellites still had to eject their films after photographing their targets. Packages of films are normally ejected over the ocean. When the capsule gets close to the surface a parachute opens to slow the flight. An aircraft is sent to pluck the package out of the air. The whole operation takes some time, though it is far quicker than using spy aircraft.

However, it has recently become possible to develop the film automatically on the satellite and then scan the film electronically. The information on the film is sent by radio signals to ground stations which translate the electronic data back into photographs. The whole process can be done so rapidly that intelligence officers can scan the photographs almost immediately after they are taken. Modern spy satellites are able to inform about events virtually while they are happening.

Espionage has become so important to the military that about 40 per cent of the military satellites launched by the superpowers are for photographic reconnaissance, and they operate in relatively low orbits, 125 miles (200 km) or so above the Earth.

Close-look Spying

Photographic reconnaissance satellites come in two varieties. One scans a large area of territory using a wide-angle, low-resolution camera. If the military intelligence agents spot something of interest to them on these photographs, a second type of reconnaissance satellite is sent to have a closer look with a high-resolution camera. The photographs taken by these close-look satellites show incredible details — not only can individual soldiers be seen but the photographs also reveal what the soldiers are doing.

Increasingly, these two operations — large-area surveillance and close-look spying — are done by one satellite. The American Big Bird satellite, for example, does both, although generally speaking the Soviets use a different satellite for each type of mission.

One task of reconnaissance satellites is to identify targets for nuclear weapons, and to allow the positions of these targets to be accurately

The Lockheed SR-71 Blackbird reconnaissance aircraft of the US Air Force. The first flight of the SR-71 was made in 1962 but the aircraft is still much used for reconnaissance. Flying at more than 80,000 feet (24,000 meters), the aircraft are virtually in space and have a view of a large area of the Earth's surface. The quality of the photographs taken is, in some circumstances, still better than the pictures that can be obtained from reconnaissance satellites.

determined. Before the age of spy satellites, the positions of targets in, say, the Soviet Union could not be discovered accurately enough — available maps were simply much too crude.

Space espionage to obtain targeting information is an essential activity for any nuclear power wishing to be independent of the superpowers. And this is why China and France have launched their own reconnaissance satellites. The UK, however, has chosen to remain dependent on information from American satellites for targeting British nuclear weapons.

Photographic satellites are not the only spies in space. There are special satellites looking at, for example, the oceans. Some ocean-surveillance satellites identify and track warships. These satellites normally use radar to do their job. The radar on a Soviet ocean spy satellite is usually powered by a small nuclear reactor carried on board. In 1978, Cosmos 954 had an accident and scattered radioactive material when the nuclear reactor burnt up as it re-entered the Earth's atmosphere. Some of the radioactivity contaminated part of Canada.

Listening to the Enemy

The most sophisticated spies in space are the electronic surveillance satellites operated by electronic intelligence, or Elint, agencies. These spacecraft carry extremely complicated equipment to collect and analyse radio signals generated by the enemy's military forces as they go about their business.

The signals of particular interest to Elint officers are those arising from radio and telephone communications between military bases, communications between military units, and communications between military units and their command centers. Also of great interest are all types of radar signals — from air-defense systems, from warships, from missile-control units, from early-warning-of-attack systems, and so on.

The purpose of electronic reconnaissance satellites is to discover the sources of electronic signals generated by the enemy's military forces and to determine the characteristics of these signals. This information is then used to help design weapons to penetrate the enemy's defenses and to produce electronic counter-measures against his weapon-systems. Given the importance of electronic warfare in today's battlefield, the electronic reconnaissance satellites are the most crucial of the spies in space.

Electronic reconnaissance satellites, orbiting 300 miles (500 km) or

so from Earth, may be the most important spies in space but American Vela satellites easily take the record in size of orbits. The mission of the Vela satellites is to detect nuclear explosions in the Earth's atmosphere and in outer space. Twelve Vela satellites have been launched but only a couple are still operational. They orbit at an altitude of about 68,000 miles (110,000 km), really deep in space.

Above: These two Dryden Flight research Center's YF-12 aircraft are being used to study the effects of extremely rapid build-ups of temperature at speeds of more than 2,000 miles an hour (3,200 km/h). The temperature of the fixture suspended under the upper aircraft is kept below zero degrees until testing is ready to begin. Explosives mixed with chemicals within the insulator are then set off to blow off the cover. Gauges inside the apparatus measure rate of heat which, at the extremely fast speeds the aircraft fly at, rapidly climbs to more than 150 degrees centigrade (300F). The information obtained is needed, among other things, to design spacecraft.

Right: The YF-12 is the world's fastest aircraft, capable of cruising at speeds of more than 2,000 miles an hour at altitudes of well over 70,000 feet (21,000 meters). The aircraft are used to collect in-flight performance data at Mach 3 speeds (3 times the speed of sound).

Right, inset: The Lockheed U-2R high altitude reconnaissance aircraft of the US Air Force in flight. This model was developed from the original U-2 which entered service in 1957. The problem with reconnaissance aircraft is the time delay between the time the aircraft takes its pictures and the time these are recovered after landing, developed and analysed. Nowadays, the military require intelligence information about events, such as enemy troop movements, as they are actually happening, or in real-time as the experts say.

Above, inset: Because of the need for real-time information, the military are most interested in satellites for reconnaissance, both photographic and electronic, and communications. This is a typical communications satellite in orbit above the Earth. This satellite has 71.5 square feet (6.6 square meters) of silicon solar cells mounted on two panels which always point to the Sun. The solar cells produce enough power (740 watts) to charge the nickel-cadmium batteries carried by the satellite to operate its communications equipment. The satellite's orbiting weight is about 1,000 pounds (450 kg). The picture also clearly shows the satellite's antennae and their reflectors.

Main picture and right, inset: Using satellites the military are able to locate, identify, and track enemy forces as they move even in their own territory. This information is used for extremely accurate target acquisition.

Left, main picture: The Tracking and Data Relay Satellite System will consist of two specialized satellites, like the one in the picture, in stationary orbit and a ground terminal located at White Sands, New Mexico. The system will relay data, commands, video and voice to and from spacecraft and the ground terminal. The system was launched into orbit by the Challenger space shuttle in April 1983. The Tracking and Data Relay Satellite System is providing tracking and communications services for up to 100 separate spacecraft.

Left, inset: The military significance of the Tracking and Data Relay Satellite System is that it allows virtually continuous communications between the ground station and military satellites even when they are on the other side of the Earth. This greatly increases the real-time capabilities of military reconnaissance and communications satellites.

Below: The function of this Vela satellite is to detect nuclear explosions in the atmosphere and outer space. A Vela satellite detected what might have been a low-yield nuclear explosion over the sea in the Indian Ocean on 22 September 1979. From an altitude of 36,000 miles (58,000 km) the Vela satellite sent a signal which was interpreted as a nuclear explosion, presumably carried out by the South Africans. Although the scientists operating the Vela system believe it was a nuclear explosion, the event is still controversial.

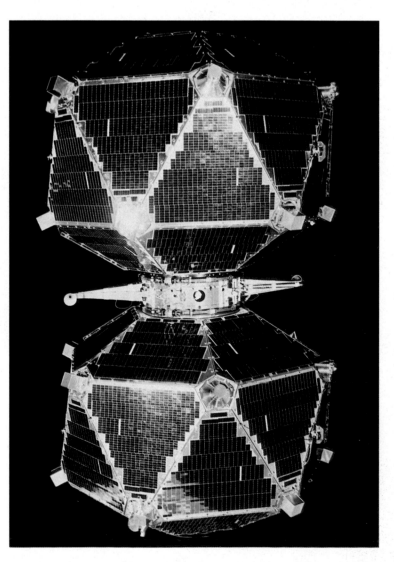

Main picture: This interesting photograph was taken from the Soviet Soyuz-22 spaceship. It shows a region of the river Vilyuy, a tributary of the Lena, 62 miles (100 km) west of Yakutsk. Such photographs are not often released by the Soviet authorities.

Below: Most of the well-known landmarks of New York City are visible in these images taken from a satellite. The five boroughs of New York are quite visible: Queens, upper right: Manhattan, center; the Bronx, top center; and Staten Island, bottom center. Across the Hudson (note the many piers) are Newark and Jersey City, Elizabeth City (note the storage tanks) to the west, and Paterson, near the upper left corner. Central Park stands out in the darker area (because of shadows from tall buildings) of Manhattan. Three airports can be seen — La Guardia on the north side of Queens, Newark International Airport north of Newark, and the third near top center. Note the cluster of boats around the Verrazano bridge (bottom center).

Below: This is a high-altitude photograph of the Washington, D.C. area taken from an aircraft flying at 50,500 feet. All the major buildings and thoroughfares of the American capital are clearly visible. Military reconnaissance satellite pictures would, of course, show much more detail. Very high resolutions are now possible. On the best military pictures it is possible to see clearly and identify, for example, aircraft on runways and to identify the activities of troops.

Below: An American satellite photograph of a wheat crop in the Ukraine, USSR. The photograph was taken at an altitude of 570 miles above the Earth. The picture, in infrared, covers an area of 110 square miles. The lake in the lower left hand corner is the Vslmlyanskoye, east of Volgograd. It is now possible to develop film automatically on satellites and electronically scan the film. The information is sent by radio to ground stations which convert it back to photographs.

Below: This is a color composite photograph taken from a US satellite at an altitude of 568 miles. The scene is the lower Volga river in the USSR. A great deal of space photography is now being done, covering the entire surface of the globe, including the oceans. Of the about 2,200 military satellites put into orbit since 1957 by the USA and the USSR, some 40 per cent are for photographic reconnaissance. New reconnaissance satellites are launched at the rate of about 40 a year.

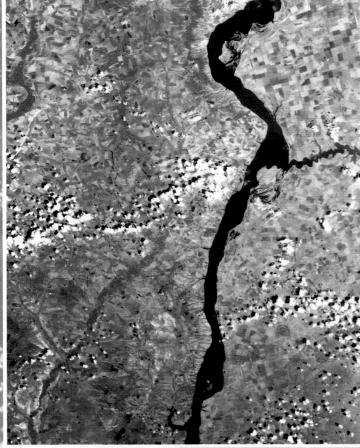

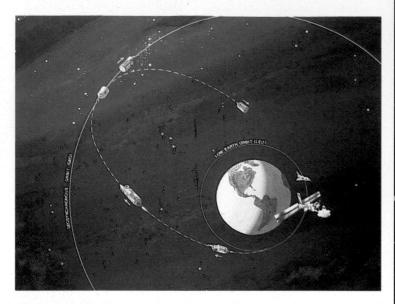

Above: An artists's impression of a space station, a space shuttle in low-earth orbit, and the propulsion of a satellite into a high orbit. The ability of the shuttle to launch satellites into such orbits will considerably increase military space capabilities.

Right, main picture and left inset: Espionage in space will be greatly facilitated by space stations which can, for example, be used for the continuous observation of enemy territory. Electronic intelligence operations will also be considerably increased by equipment carried on space stations. Of particular importance is the monitoring of electronic signals generated by military forces. Each side is very anxious to listen in to the other side's radio and telephone communications between military bases, army units, and so on. Electronic intelligence also includes monitoring civilian and diplomatic telephone and other communications. Electronic intelligence is already a vast and costly enterprise using, as well as satellites, global land, sea, and air information-gathering operations. In future warfare, electronics will reign supreme. The 'electronic order of battle' will determine the outcome of battles. New offensive and defensive weapons relying on a variety of sensors are stimulating a never-ending electronic arms race to develop counter-measures, counter-counter-measures, and so on. The knowledge gained by electronic intelligence is used to develop such measures to frustrate the enemy's weapon systems. Information from satellites will play an increasing role in this electronic warfare.

Far right, inset: Soviet cosmonaut G. Beregovoi preparing a portable television camera for a TV report from space.

42

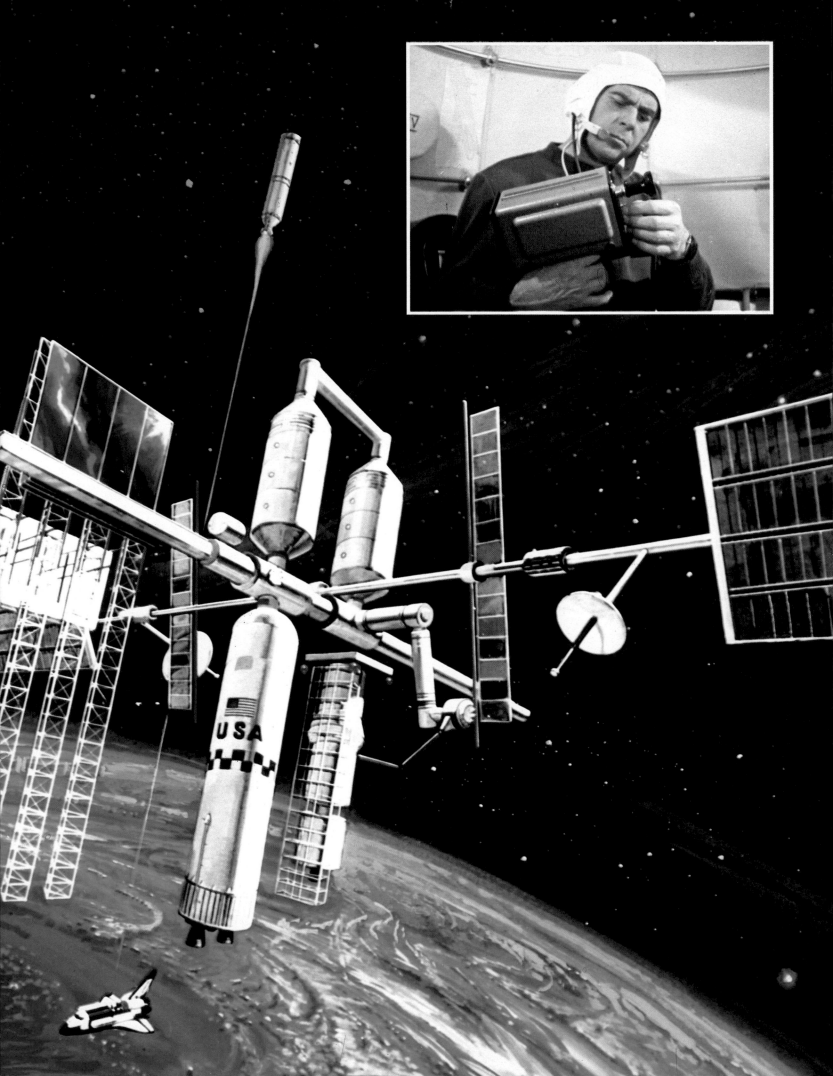

CHAPTER 3

ANTI-SATELLITE WEAPONS

The USA and the USSR are both trying to develop weapons to shoot down the other side's satellites in space. Satellites are now so crucial in military operations that they would be very high priority targets indeed in a war between the superpowers.

Hunter-Killers

A typical Soviet anti-satellite weapon is, in fact, another satellite, called a hunter-killer or interceptor satellite. The hunter-killer is launched into an orbit that will take it close to the enemy satellite that is its target. When the Soviet hunter-killer is at its closest point to its target it explodes and destroys the enemy satellite.

Soviet tests with targets and interceptor satellites began in earnest as long ago as 1967. Apparently, the last Soviet test of an anti-satellite weapon took place in mid-June 1982.

At about 15.00 on 18th June, 1982, the Soviet satellite Cosmos 1379 was launched from the space-launch center at Tyuratam. Cosmos 1379 was a hunter-killer; its mission was to seek out and destroy its target, Cosmos 1375, which had been launched on 6th June from Plesetsk.

The hunter-killer intercepted its prey during its second orbit of the Earth. When it got close to its target, the killer satellite received a signal from its command center on Earth. It headed back towards Earth, entered the Earth's atmosphere and burnt up. Its mission had been successfully carried out; if the signal from the command center had instructed it to, Cosmos 1379 could have exploded and destroyed the target satellite. This is, of course, exactly what would have happened in a war.

Cosmos 1379 was about the fiftieth hunter-killer launched in the Soviet anti-satellite weapon program. The bulk of the interceptor satellites were launched from Tyuratam; most of the target satellites were launched from Plesetsk.

In many of these tests the interceptor was exploded with conventional explosives to test its capability to destroy the target satellite. In other tests, the hunter-killer satellite was taken close to the target satellite and, like Cosmos 1379, commanded back to Earth to be burnt up in the atmosphere. There is no point in destroying very expensive target satellites unnecessarily.

Typically, a Soviet hunter-killer satellite is maneuvered, by signals from the command center in the USSR, towards its target. The interceptor then uses its own on-board radar to make the final approach towards the target.

American ASATs

The Americans have developed a different type of anti-satellite weapon from the Soviet one. It consists of a small missile launched into space from a converted F-15 Eagle fighter aircraft flying at a very high altitude, of more than 70,000 feet (21,000 meters). The missile, which may carry a warhead filled with a conventional explosive, is guided close to the enemy satellite. The warhead is then released and guides itself onto the target using a sensor in its nose. The sensor is able to pick up and home in on the infra-red radiation given off by the enemy

Much is known about US space shuttle activities but very little is published about Soviet activities in this field. It was reported in 1978, however, that the USSR had carried out unmanned atmospheric tests of its delta-winged reusable manned space vehicle. The craft was launched from a Bear bomber. The USSR later confirmed it was indeed developing a reusable spacecraft. US reconnaissance satellites have observed the construction of a long runway at Tyuratam; the Soviet space launch center. It is generally believed that this will be used by the Soviet space shuttle. The picture shows an impression of the complex at Tyuratam.

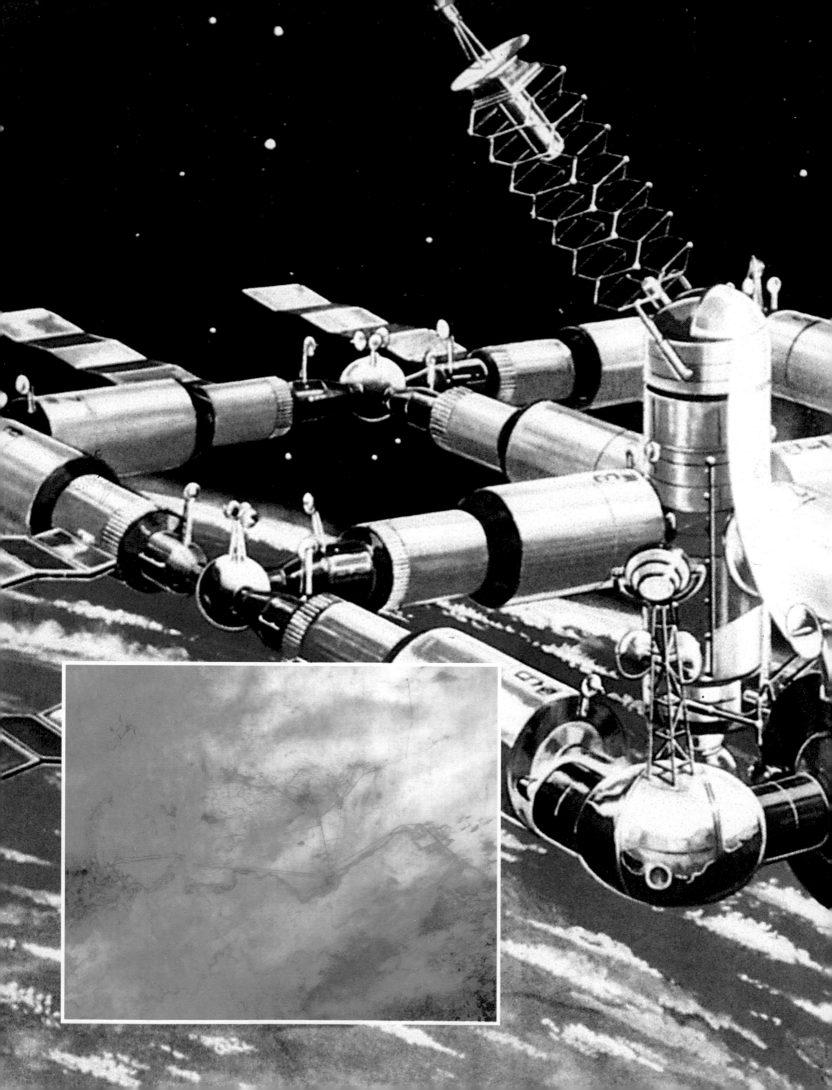

satellite. The warhead either explodes when it is close to the target or makes a direct hit on it. The US Air Force first tested its anti-satellite missile in January 1984.

One direct hit on a satellite from a relatively small warhead traveling fast would disable the satellite. The warhead does not even need to explode if it is accurate. The Americans are developing a non-explosive maneuvering warhead for its anti-satellite weapons, known as the Miniature Homing Intercept Vehicle. A number of such vehicles could be launched into orbit by a rocket and released near a Soviet satellite. Alternatively, the vehicle could be launched by missiles carried by F-15 aircraft.

Each maneuverable vehicle carries an infra-red sensor that guides it to the enemy satellite. The vehicle then rams the target satellite at high speed and disables it.

Because satellites can be so easily damaged by small things hitting it, one type of anti-satellite weapon under active consideration simply discharges a cloud of ball-bearings, or small pellets, in the path of an enemy satellite. The target satellite is disabled when it flies through the cloud.

The killer satellites so far developed and tested are effective only against enemy satellites in relatively low orbits. These satellites include some used for reconnaissance but also those used to support strategic nuclear submarines operating in the seas close to the enemy homeland.

The USA is very concerned about Soviet strategic nuclear submarines operating close to its shores. Ballistic missiles fired from these submarines could reach their targets in minutes rather than the half-hour or so taken by intercontinental ballistic missiles fired at the USA from sites in the Soviet Union.

To counter this threat, the US Air Force intends to arm several of its units with anti-satellite weapons capable of attacking the low-orbit Soviet satellites supporting Soviet strategic nuclear submarines.

Attacking in High Orbits

Although both the USA and the USSR have developed anti-satellite weapons that are effective against enemy satellites in low orbits, neither have yet managed to knock out satellites in very high orbits. Both sides would dearly like to be able to do so. In particular, they would like to be able to attack the other side's communications and early-warning-of-attack satellites in geostationary orbits, about 22,000 miles (35,000 km) above the Earth.

These satellites move so as to remain always above the same point on the Earth's surface. To attack them would require high-energy laser weapons, of the type envisaged for a 'Star Wars' defense. Both sides are trying to develop laser weapons, which are described in the next chapter. If they are to succeed they will need to develop compact sources of power to provide the energy for the lasers.

A possible power supply for a high-energy laser in space is a nuclear reactor. The Soviets have been orbiting small nuclear reactors for a decade or so. And the US plans to put a larger nuclear reactor into space in the near future. We must expect nuclear activity in space to increase in future years.

Inset: This satellite picture shows the launch sites at Tyuratam. By 1981, the major roads leading to the main runway were completed and the runway was extended in length to about 4 miles (6 km). The runway is now about the same as the runway used by the Americans for their space shuttle. Soviet manned flights in a reusable launcher are expected to begin soon.

Main picture: Soviet space shuttle flights may be used to construct a manned space station, probably using a modular design like the one illustrated. It seems though that the first Soviet shuttle vehicle will be smaller than its American counterpart, probably weighing about 18 tons. This vehicle would probably carry payloads of about 15 tons, about a half that of the American shuttle. But both superpowers are likely to develop heavy-lift vehicles capable of carrying materials into space for the construction of large space stations.

47

Above: This is the view of the Soviet Tyuratam space center seen from the US shuttle. It is from this center that some of the Soviet hunter-killer satellites are launched.

Right: An artist's impression of a Soviet orbital anti-satellite weapon. If one of the superpowers ever decided to make a surprise attack on the other the first thing it would want to do would be to destroy the other side's reconnaissance satellites, which, as we have seen, are the military's eyes and ears in space. As time goes on, the military are becoming more and more dependent on satellites for intelligence and target acquisition, and for command, control, and communications in war. Also, navigation and meteorological satellites play a crucial military role in improving the performance of weapons. It is no wonder that satellites of all types have become prime military targets on both sides.

Main picture: Anti-satellite warfare is one of a very few military fields in which the USSR seems to be ahead of the USA. The Americans are, however, catching up fast. This photograph shows an American anti-satellite weapon on an F-15 combat aircraft. This weapon is somewhat more sophisticated than Soviet anti-satellite systems. The American missile is guided by on-board sensors close to an enemy satellite and the warhead released. A sensor in the warhead itself is able to pick up infra-red radiation given off by the satellite and home on to it. The warhead may make a direct hit on the target and destroy it. Alternatively, the warhead may explode when it is close to the enemy satellite.

Far left, inset: F-15 in flight, carrying an anti-satellite missile. The aircraft will release the missile at an altitude of over 70,000 feet (21,000 meters) so that it can travel into space and attack a target satellite. It can be seen that the missile is quite small. Some years ago, the USA deployed a ground-based anti-satellite system using the US Army's Nike-Zeus missiles. The system was, however, soon abandoned.

Left inset: The homing head of the American anti-satellite missile. The US anti-satellite system could become fully operational in the second half of the 1980s.

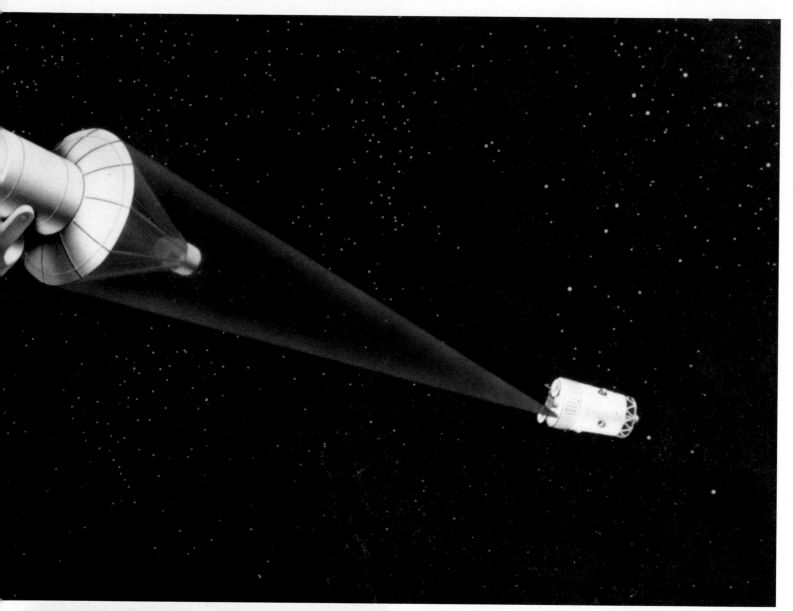

Above: In addition to the more conventional types of anti-satellite weapons, both superpowers are developing lasers for possible use in anti-satellite weapons. Current US plans are to develop for military use lasers with power outputs of up to 5 million watts. A laser weapon half as powerful as this could easily destroy a fast-moving aircraft or an air-to-air missile, let alone an enemy satellite. This artist's impression of a US laser anti-satellite weapon shows how a rotating mirror would be used to target the laser beam.

Far left: A space laser weapon must be able precisely to point a high-energy laser beam at a vulnerable spot on the enemy satellite. This photograph shows the Talon Gold experiment in which target-acquisition equipment is tested by flying it on the space shuttle. The Talon Gold system uses a laser radar to acquire the target and is being developed jointly by NASA's Jet Propulsion Laboratory and Lockheed Missiles and Space Corporation.

Left: A typical satellite target for an anti-satellite weapon. It must be remembered that satellites need ground stations through which to transmit information. These ground stations tend to be large and are more vulnerable to attack than the satellites themselves. Both superpowers are, therefore, trying to make their satellites more independent of ground stations.

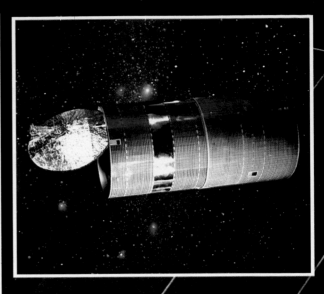

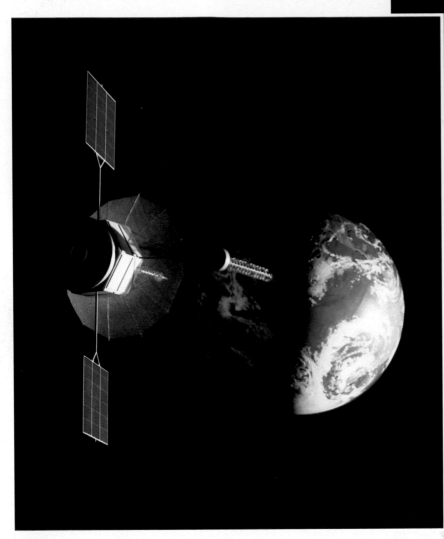

Above and inset; Efforts are being made to make satellites, such as the communications satellites pictured above, less vulnerable to attack. Satellites are, for example, being hardened against damage produced by the electro-magnetic pulse from a nuclear explosion in space. Such a nuclear explosion would release a very large amount of electro-magnetic radiation. When this hit a satellite it would produce large voltages in the electronic components used in the satellite's equipment. This voltage pulse could easily wreck the electronics and make the satellite useless. Satellites may also be hardened against attack by laser beams. Another possibility is to supply a satellite with equipment to warn it of the approach of an enemy satellite and to enable it to take evasive action when attacked by an intercepter. Satellites may also be put very deep into space so that they are virtually invisible. The satellites would remain inactive until a signal was sent to them to move from the depths of space into orbits closer to the Earth and start their missions. Yet another way of making satellites less vulnerable to attack would be to deploy in space a large number of decoys so that an enemy would not know which space object to attack.

Main picture: Some satellites, like this meteorological satellite, are large and particularly vulnerable to attack. Some of the equipment which can be seen on the satellite is very fragile.

Left inset: Satellites will become more vulnerable to attack when space stations are deployed. These stations could carry anti-satellite weapons. The stations would, of course, themselves be vulnerable to attack and need their own defences.

Main picture and below: Spacecraft are used to observe the development and progress of conflicts wherever they occur in the world. They could, therefore, be used to manage crises. Satellites also play an important role in verifying that countries are fulfilling their obligations under arms control treaties. At present, the capability to carry out crises-management and verification activities by satellites is only in the hands of the USA and the USSR. France has, however, proposed that an international satellite agency should be set up so that future spacecraft could be used to help settle international disputes. They could also help the United Nations in its peace-keeping activities. Already, spacecraft are planned for use in natural disasters in the Search and Rescue Satellite System. Initially, the system will be used to locate ship and aircraft distress signals anywhere in the world.

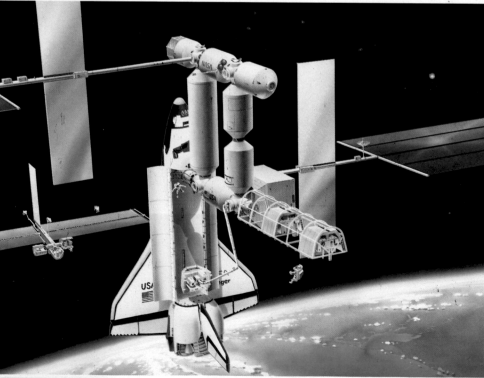

CHAPTER 4

STAR WARS

The space-based 'Star Wars' defense system that President Reagan believes could render nuclear weapons obsolete is a complicated one. It envisages several layers of different types of weapons stretching from the ground to deep outer space. Each layer would be designed to attack Soviet missiles fired at the United States during different parts of the Soviet missiles' flight path. A 'Star Wars' defense would move America's frontiers into deep space.

Conflict in Deep Space

The topmost defense layer would attack the Soviet missiles just after they were launched and while they were still in the Earth's atmosphere — in other words, before they went into space. The Soviet missiles that got through this first defense layer would be attacked in space by weapons in the second layer. The third layer would deal with any surviving Soviet warheads as they left space and re-entered the Earth's atmosphere.

The weapons in the first defense layer would include high-energy lasers on space battle-stations. Other space battle-stations would carry lasers to attack Soviet missiles while they were in space. The third layer of defense would consist of American anti-ballistic missiles fired from the ground.

These anti-ballistic missiles would be capable of exceptionally high speeds; they would travel so fast that they would be able to intercept enemy missiles at high altitudes in the Earth's atmosphere before these missiles could reach their targets in the USA. Very large complicated radar sets would track the Soviet missiles and guide the American anti-ballistic missiles to them.

Laser Battle Stations

Another system that has been suggested by American military scientists for attacking Soviet missiles in flight consists of a laser weapon built in a station on the top of a high mountain, say 16,000 feet (5,000 meters) or more above the ground. A large mirror would be launched into a space orbit to reflect the laser beam fired from the mountain top and to aim the laser beam at the enemy missile.

A laser weapon capable of producing sufficient energy to damage a missile enough to make it useless would need to be very heavy. To launch such a weight into space would be expensive and difficult. Putting the system on Earth on a mountain top would avoid these problems. Earth-based lasers would also, of course, be easier to repair and maintain than space-based ones.

A major problem with using lasers as weapons is that when the light in a laser beam travels through air it doesn't stay in a small beam; the beam tends to spread out. Broad laser beams would be much less efficient at damaging missiles than narrow ones. One of the attractions of putting lasers into space is that there is no air in space to broaden the beam and so the beam remains narrowly focused. Putting the laser on a high mountain, above much of the atmosphere, is another way of reducing the problem of transmitting the beam through the air.

A close-up of a discharge in the laser laboratory of the US Air Force's weapons laboratory at Kirtland Air Force Base, New Mexico. Some anti-ballistic missile and anti-satellite weapon systems are based on high-energy lasers. The idea is that a laser-beam weapon is capable of delivering a much higher and more accurate concentration of firepower than any other weapon. This, it is argued, can be used to destroy enemy weapons, like nuclear warheads in space.

Advocates of the 'Star Wars' idea say that about fifty space battle-stations would be enough to protect all parts of the USA from an attack by Soviet missiles, provided that each battle-station carried very powerful lasers. Other scientists disagree and insist that far more battle-stations would be required.

Each space battle-station would carry equipment and computers to detect and identify enemy ballistic missiles as they are launched. This equipment would also work out the path of each missile and aim the high-energy laser at it.

The space battle would be controlled from the ground from a command center which would contain the main computer. The command center would receive information from a set of satellites that would detect enemy missiles just after they had been launched. These early-warning satellites are, in fact, in orbit today.

As soon as the command center had been informed by the early-warning satellites of an enemy missile attack, it would activate the space battle-stations. And then the space battle would begin.

X-ray Lasers

Some military scientists want to use lasers based on X-rays in space weapons instead of lasers using light. X-ray lasers would make much more powerful weapons for attacking enemy missiles than ordinary lasers; they would also be smaller and lighter. The snag is that the X-rays for a space-based laser weapon would have to be produced from a nuclear explosion in space.

X-ray lasers have been tested by American scientists at the underground nuclear-weapon test site in Nevada. It is reported that the Soviets are also experimenting with high-energy laser systems, including X-ray lasers.

The US has already tested some laser weapons on Earth. For example, in 1978 the US Navy destroyed a missile in flight with a laser weapon. In 1983, the Airborne Laser Laboratory, operated by the US Air Force, showed that Sidewinder air-to-air missiles can be shot down in flight by laser weapons, carried by an aeroplane, at ranges of between 5 and 10 miles (8 and 16 km). The airborne laboratory shot down all five Sidewinder missiles fired at it from another aircraft. It is believed that new Soviet battleships are being equipped with high-energy laser weapons to defend them against attacks by enemy cruise missiles.

But none of the lasers so far tested are anywhere near powerful enough to destroy ballistic missiles in space. Therefore, great efforts are being made in both the USA and the USSR to increase the power of laser weapons.

American military scientists are developing a large mirror, 13 ft (4 meters) in diameter, to steer a high-energy laser beam in space. And in the Talon Gold project technologies for aiming laser weapons at enemy ballistic missiles are being investigated.

American government scientists are enthusiastic about the 'Star Wars' idea and believe that an effective system can be put into space early next century. Other scientists doubt that the technology can be developed. Only time, and a lot more money, will tell who is right.

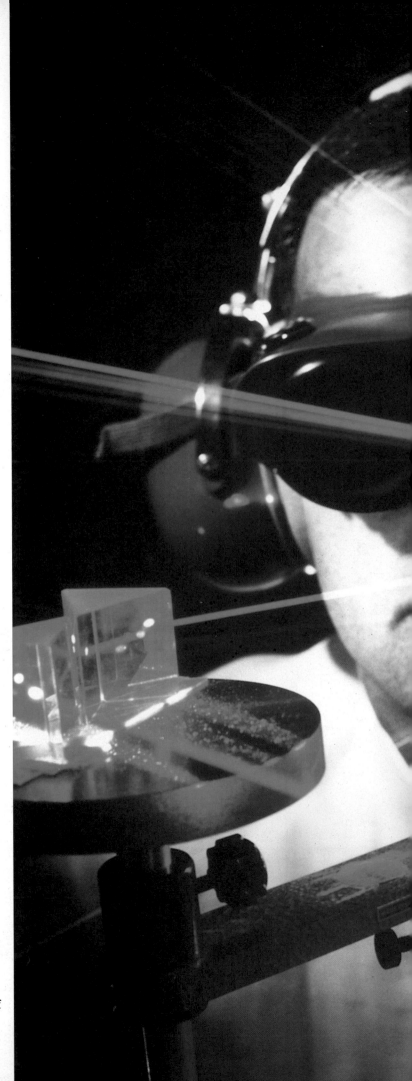

A scientist operating an argon laser at a laboratory at the Hughes Aircraft Company. Laser beams travel at the speed of light – 186,000 miles per second – very much faster than a missile can travel. Enthusiasts believe that large chemical high-energy laser weapons for deployment in ground stations, such as on a mountain top, could be developed within five years. Other scientists say that this is an over-optimistic forecast and that there are many serious problems to be overcome. Some scientists doubt the feasibility of the large-scale use of high-energy laser weapons.

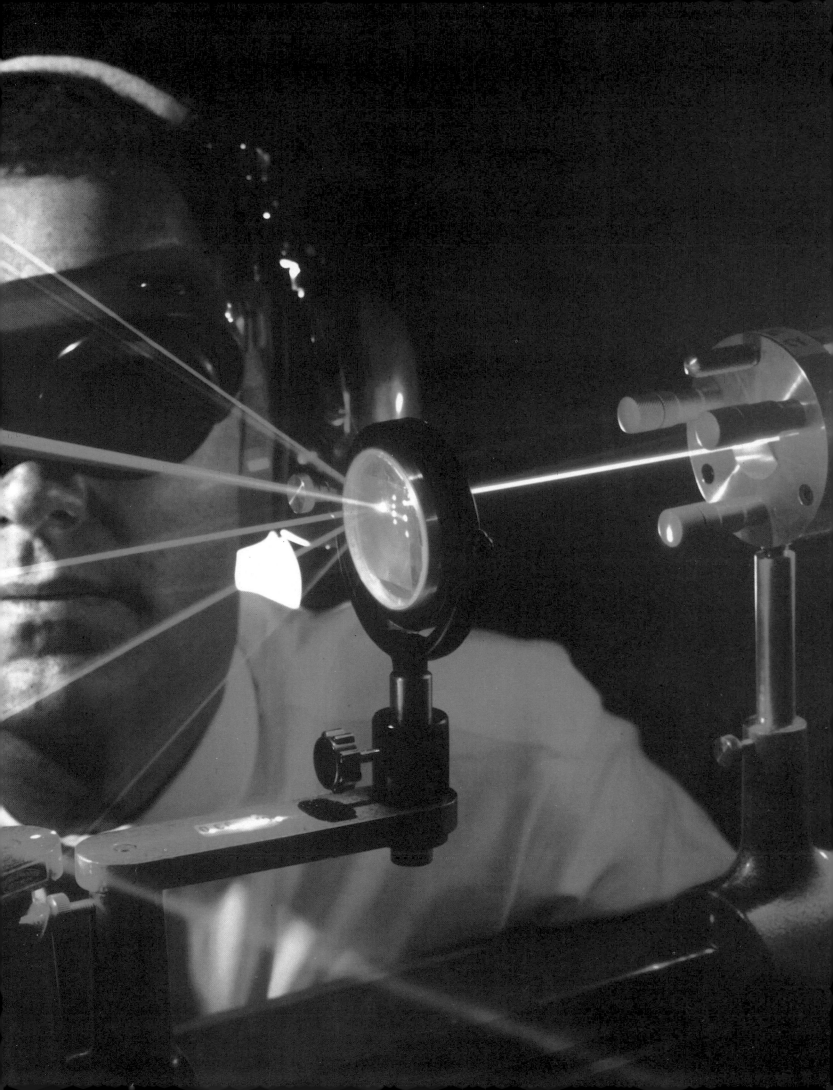

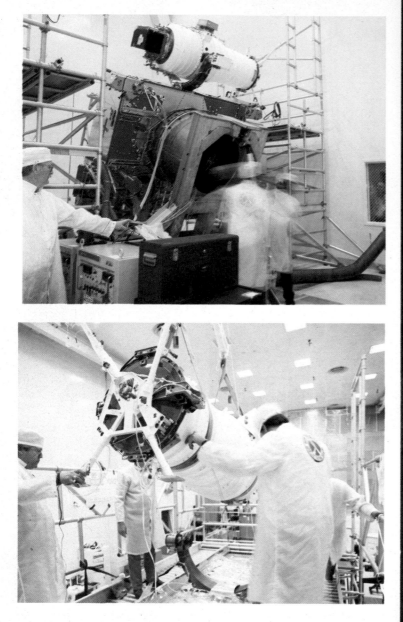

Above, top and bottom: The Teal Ruby experiment is to develop an infra-red telescope to detect enemy aircraft and missiles. These pictures show the telescope sensor and the pointing mechanism of the telescope aboard the spacecraft which will carry it into space. The US Defense Advanced Research Project Agency is developing elements of a space-based laser-weapon system under the other code-name Talon Gold and LODE. Talon Gold uses a laser radar system to achieve the required accuracy for identifying and tracking enemy weapons — such as ballistic missile warheads — and pointing the laser beam. LODE, Large Optics Demonstration Experiment, is trying to develop and test a complex mirror to focus and direct the laser beam onto the enemy weapon. The current experiment involves a mirror, 13 feet (4 metres) in diameter, to focus and steer the laser beam. These systems, if successful, are likely to be deployed on space battle-stations. The development of these systems is expensive. The US has already spent about $4 billion on high-energy lasers and plans to spend a great deal more. The USSR is also devoting large resources of money and scientific manpower to develop laser weapons.

Main picture: An impression of a Teal Ruby infra-red telescope on station in space.

Right inset: Pictures of an aircraft being destroyed by a laser beam.

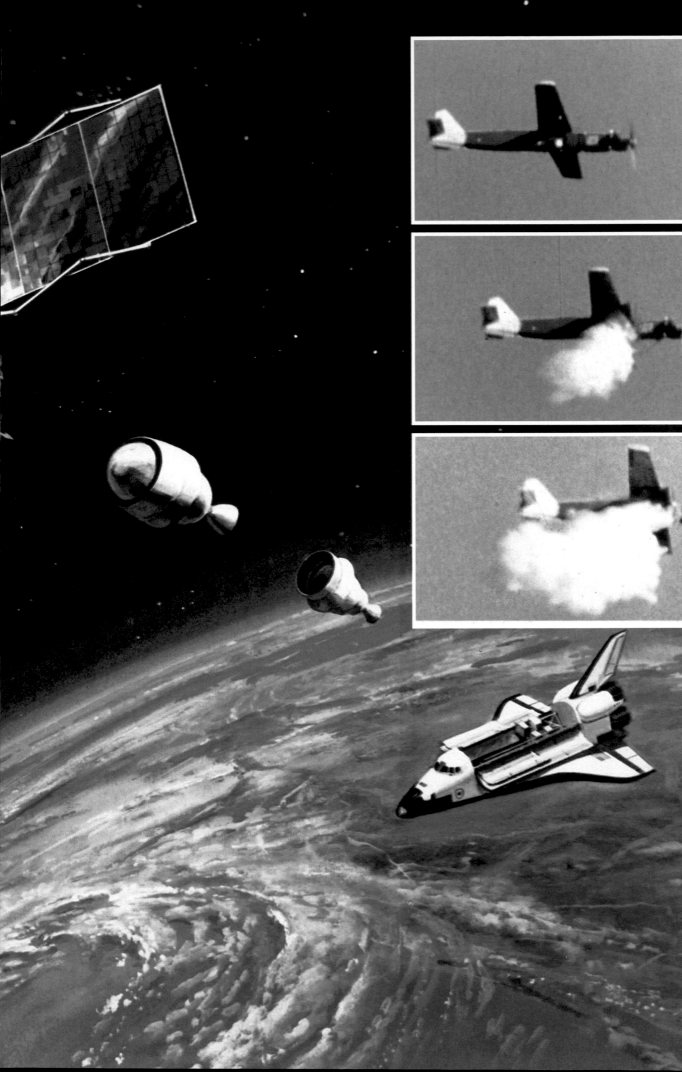

Above: A chemical laser mounted on a US Marine Corps armored vehicle, used as a mobile test unit. In 1976, a laser on the mobile test unit destroyed aircraft at the Redstone Arsenal in Alabama.

Below: The US Air Force Airborne Laser Laboratory is a modified Boeing NKC-135 aircraft used to support high-energy laser research by the US Air Force Weapons Laboratory at Kirtland Air Force Base, New Mexico. The aircraft is equipped with a chemical (carbon dioxide) laser. The airborne laboratory has used its laser to attack Sidewinder air-to-air missiles fired at it from other aircraft.

Right: An artist's impression of an American laser battle-station in space. The station would be designed to attack Soviet ballistic missiles soon after they were fired or to engage the warheads from these missiles as they passed through space. To engage a large number of warheads in space (the Soviets currently have about 8,000 nuclear warheads deployed on strategic ballistic missiles) would require a large number of battle-stations. Many scientists believe that it is not technologically feasible to provide an effective space-based laser defense. Be this as it may, the cost of developing and deploying such a system would be enormous. Clearly, only the two superpowers could contemplate spending such huge sums of money.

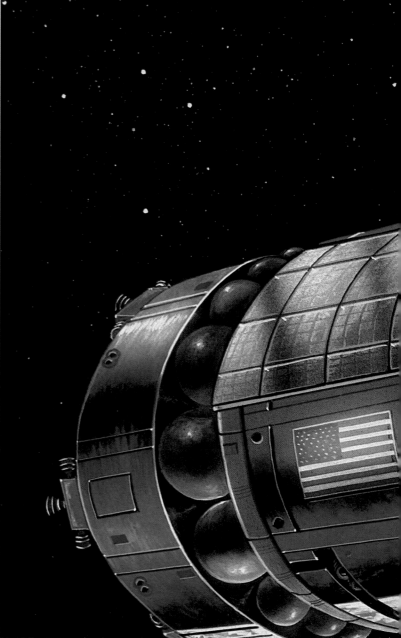

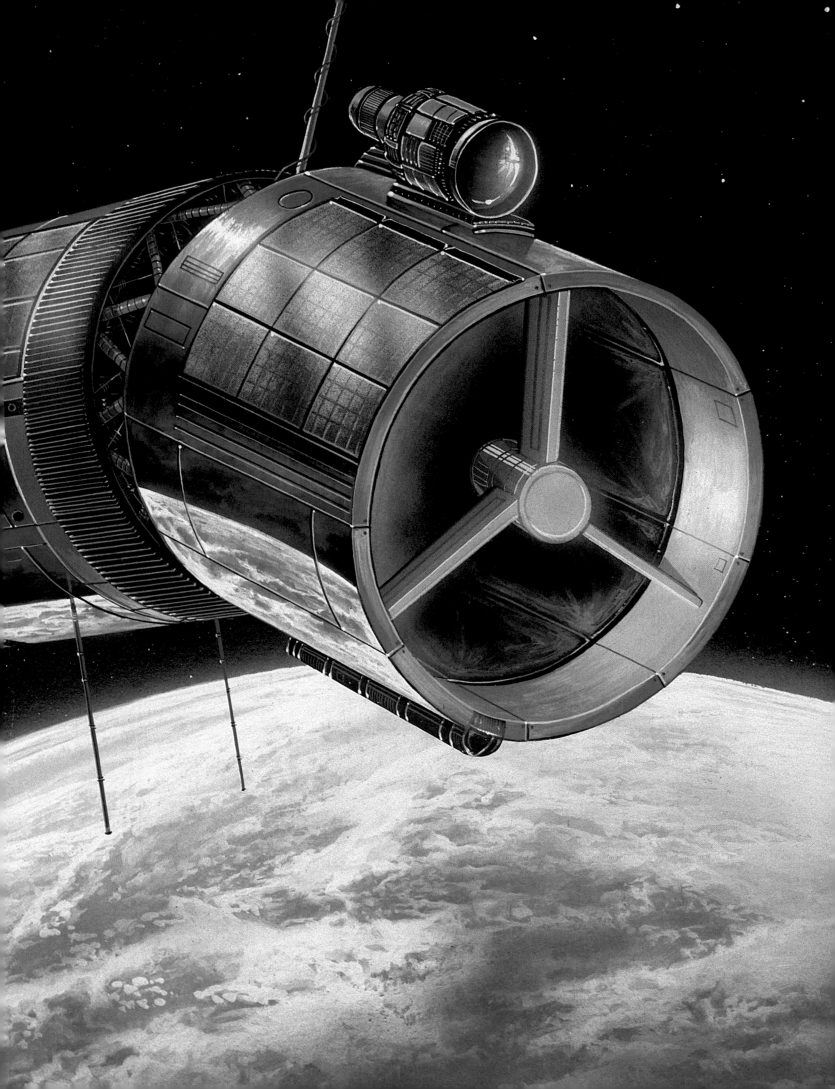

Right: In an anti-ballistic missile system, enemy warheads that survive the high-energy laser weapons in space would be attacked by missiles fired at them from the ground. These ground-based anti-ballistic missiles would have exceptionally high accelerations and would be guided to the enemy missiles by complex radars. An anti-ballistic missile would carry a nuclear warhead. When the missile came close to the in-coming enemy warhead its warhead would explode and destroy the enemy warhead. The interception would take place outside the Earth's atmosphere.

Above: The US Army is testing non-nuclear warheads as possible weapons against attacking enemy missiles. The program, to develop warheads for ground-based anti-ballistic missiles, is called the Homing Overlay Experiment, or HOE. This picture shows the warhead. The device has a number of metal ribs, about seven feet long and seeded with steel weights. The ribs are wound around the neck of the HOE warhead during flight. They unfurl seconds before the HOE warhead collides with a target ballistic missile warhead and destroys it.

Above right, inset: The HOE warhead streaks upwards in a test. Minutes later it succeeded in destroying its target, a re-entry vehicle from a ballistic missile fired from the Vandenberg Air Force Base, California.

Far right: The anti-ballistic missile carrying HOE rises from its launch pad at the Kwajalein Missile Range.

Left: The construction of space battle-stations for high-energy laser weapons will require much effort by astronauts. This picture shows an astronaut in space wearing a nitrogen-propelled manned maneuvering unit (MMU) which enables him to become independent of the mother ship, in this case the space shuttle Challenger. With the MMU, the spaceman can move around and perform tasks, such as constructing platforms in space. The astronaut is equipped with two cameras — one attached to his MMU and a TV camera on his helmet.

Above: Another astronaut practising movements in space. With regular space shuttle flights many astronauts will be trained to operate in space.

Below: A possible task for future astronauts is servicing satellites such as the one depicted in this picture. The satellite carries a Teal Ruby telescope to detect and track enemy aircraft or missiles in flight. The spacecraft would be equipped with computers to work out the trajectories of enemy missiles and aim anti-ballistic missile weapons, such as high-energy lasers, at them. A ground-based command center would control a set of such satellites and direct the space battle. Such Star Wars concepts elevate war to new technological levels unthinkable a few years ago.

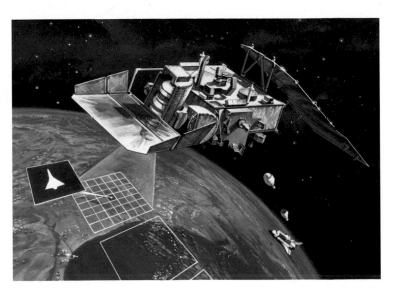

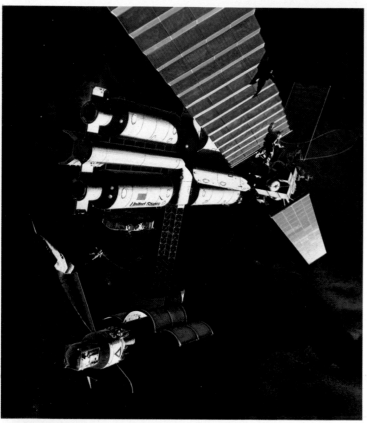

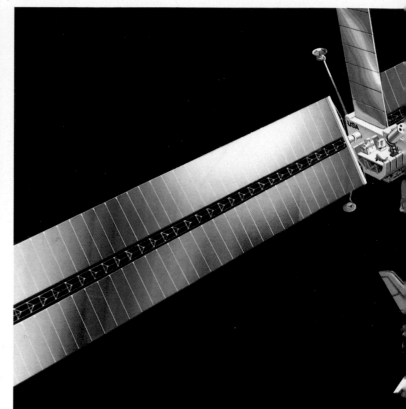

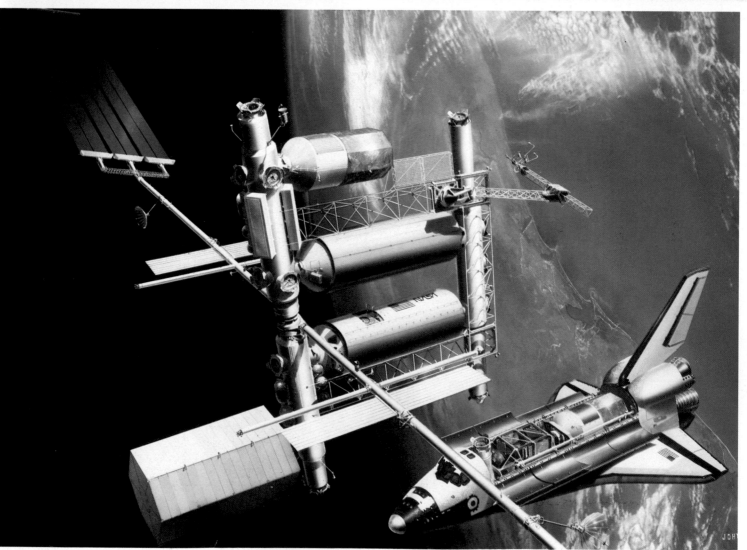

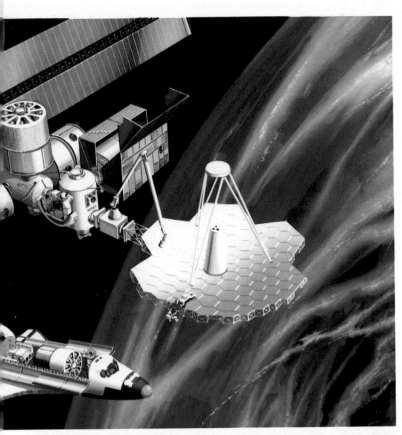

Far left: A study for NASA has produced this plan for a space station. In this concept, station control and operations are conducted from the central vertical module. With attached solar arrays, thermal radiators and communications, the central module would be the first placed in orbit, by a space shuttle. Subsequent shuttles would add passages, the four main modules, truss structure docks, and various viewing payloads. Military uses of the station may include satellite launching and repair, the deployment of anti-ballistic missile weapons and reconnaissance.

Below left: A space shuttle orbiter visits a Space Operations Center. The cylinders, with the connecting passageway, would serve as the command control center and living quarters. The service modules, brought up from Earth by shuttles and connected in space, would have the life support systems, power unit, communications apparatus, an airlock, and a docking berth for the shuttle. Potential military uses are a major stimulus for developing such space stations.

Left: A somewhat more sophisticated space station for deployment in space in the 1990s. A number of people on, say, 90-day missions, would live in modules installed in the berthing ports of the platform. As modules were added crew sizes would be increased to provide a manned permanent presence in space. Two astronauts can be seen at one end of the platform constructing a communications satellite.

Below: Most space scientists and engineers hope that future space stations like this one will be part of a technology for peace rather than a technology for war.

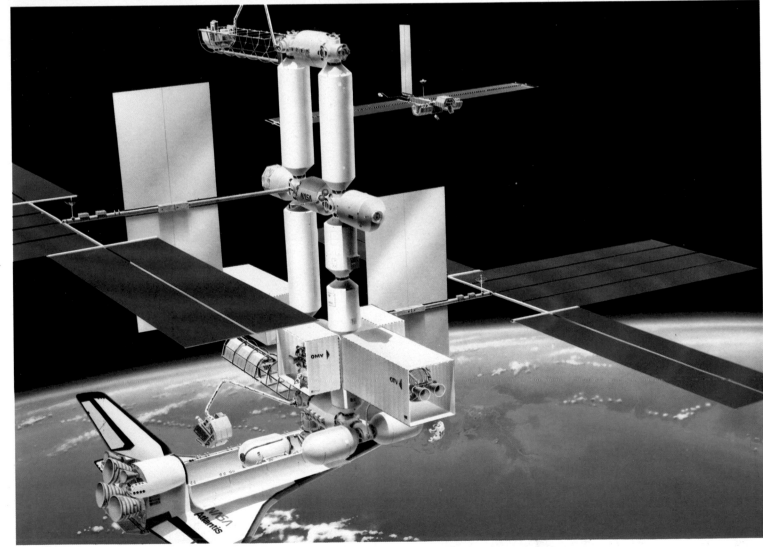

PICTURE CREDITS

Aerospatiale, Paris MARS 22 inset top, 66 bottom **Ballistic Missile Organisation** MARS 67 **Boeing Aerospace Company** MARS 19 **Daily Telegraph Colour Library** Steve Stint contents, 8 inset, 15 bottom, 25 right, 26 inset, 27 inset, 28 left, 36-37, 37 inset, 39 inset left, 39 right, 46 inset, 48, 54 left, 54 inset right, 54-55, 62-63, 64-65, endpaper **Dept. of Defense, Washington** MARS 44-45, 46-47, 48-49, 52-53, 66 top, 67 inset **Ford Aerospace and Communications Corporation** 15 top **Hughes Aircraft Company** MARS 60-61 **Lockheed California Corporation** MARS 32-33, 35 inset **Lockheed Missiles and Space Co. Inc.** MARS 20, 52 bottom, 70 top left **MARS** 16 top, 18, 53 bottom **Martin Marietta Aerospace** MARS 22 inset bottom **MacClancey Collection** NASA 1, 8-9, 12, 13, 14 inset, 14, 34, 35, 36 inset, 38-39, 40 inset right, 40 inset left, 69 top, back cover, USAF 18 inset **McDonnell Douglas Corporation** MARS 50 inset, 50-51 **NASA** 11 bottom, 16 center, 24-25, 26-27, 28-29, 30-31, 40 inset left, 40 inset right, 57 inset, 68-69, 70 bottom, 70-71, MARS 10, John C. Olson 17 **Novosti Press Agency** 40-41, 43 inset **Science Photo Library** NASA 22-23, 30 inset, 31 right, 42 left, 42 inset right, 56 inset **Societés Nationales Industrielles** MARS 21 right **Rockwell International** 11 top, 16 bottom, 42-43, 56-57, 62 top left, 62 bottom left **Frank Spooner Pictures** 6-7, 72 **US Air Force** MARS 51, 57-58, 63 inset top, center, bottom, 64 bottom, 69 bottom **US Marine Corps** MARS 64 top **US Navy** MARS 21 left **Young Artists** Colin Hay front cover, Bob Layzell 2-3

Multimedia Publications have endeavored to observe the legal requirements with regard to the rights of suppliers of photographic material.